My Daily Meditations

Dr Michael H Yeager

Copyright © 2015 **_Dr Michael H Yeager_**

All rights reserved.

ISBN: 1507840373
ISBN-13: 9781507840375

DEDICATION

I would like to dedicate this **meditation** book to my daughter Stephanie Joy Yeager who wanted me to do this project years ago for her own spiritual development and growth. This particular **meditation** book is not just for her though, but all of those who want to grow spiritually in the kingdom of God. This book should be likened unto the Royal jelly which is fed to the Queen bees in order to bring about their wonderful transformation. The word of God when it is **meditated** upon and hidden in our heart will bring about an amazing transformation within our hearts, our minds and every part of our lives. Yes you could've easily looked up the Scriptures on your own, but for some strange reason you decided to purchase this book. May it be a wonderful blessing to you and your loved ones!

CONTENTS

	Acknowledgments	i
1	**Foundational Scriptures**	3
2	**JESUS CHRIST**	11
3	*The Divine Nature*	21
4	*CONTINUED FRUITS*	35
5	*DIVINE HEALING*	49
6	*DIVINE GUIDANCE*	61
7	*AUTHORITY & POWER*	71
8	*FAITH, TRUST, BELIEVE,*	79
9	*MANY PROMISES*	91
10	*IMPORTANT SCRIPTURES*	99

ACKNOWLEDGMENTS

All of the Scriptures used in this meditation book is from the original 1611 version of the King James Bible. I give thanks to God the Father , Jesus Christ and the Holy Ghost for the powerful impact the word has had upon my life. Without the word Quicken in my heart by the Holy Ghost I would've been lost and I'm done. To the Lord of Heaven and Earth I am eternally indebted for his great love and his mercy, his protections and his provisions, his divine guidance and overwhelming goodness. To him be glory and praise for ever and ever: Amen . Most of the Scriptures you're about to read in this book are ones that I had memorized the meditated on, on a daily basis, ever sense I gave my heart to Christ in 1975

CHAPTER ONE
FOUNDATIONAL SCRIPTURES

There are some basic foundational Scriptures that you should memorize in order to grasp the reality of what God's word will do when it is hidden in a your heart. I would strongly suggest that before you proceed much further in this meditation book that you memorize these first five particular Scriptures and begin to meditate upon them. when I use the word meditate I am referring to speaking them to yourself, muttering over and over slowly allowing the Holy Spirit to quicken these words to your heart. There must be a quickening of the Scriptures in order for there to be faith to bring to pass that which you are speaking. Psalms 119 is a wonderful declaration of the quickening of God's word.

Foundational Scriptures

*Psalm 1:1 Blessed is the man that walketh not in the counsel of the ungodly, nor standeth in the way of sinners, nor sitteth in the seat of the scornful.2 But his delight is in the law of the Lord; and in his law doth he meditate day and night.3 And he shall be like a tree planted by the rivers of water, that bringeth forth his fruit in his season; his leaf also shall not wither; and whatsoever he doeth shall prosper.

---

*Joshua 1:8 This book of the law shall not depart out of thy mouth; but thou shalt meditate therein day and night, that thou mayest observe to do according to all that is written therein: for then thou shalt make thy way prosperous, and then thou shalt have good success. 9 Have not I commanded thee? Be strong and of a good courage; be not afraid, neither be thou dismayed: for the Lord thy God is with thee whithersoever thou goest.

---

*Jeremiah 15:16 Thy words were found, and I did eat them; and thy word was unto me the joy and rejoicing of mine heart: for I am called by thy name, O Lord God of hosts.

*Proverbs 4:20 My son, attend to my words; incline thine ear unto my sayings.21 Let them not depart from thine eyes; keep them in the midst of thine heart.22 For they are life unto those that find them, and health to all their flesh.

*John 15:6 If a man abide not in me, he is cast forth as a branch, and is withered; and men gather them, and cast them into the fire, and they are burned. 7 If ye abide in me, and my words abide in you, ye shall ask what ye will, and it shall be done unto you. 8 Herein is my Father glorified, that ye bear much fruit; so shall ye be my disciples.

Scriptures on meditation

*Psalm 19:14 Let the words of my mouth, and the meditation of my heart, be acceptable in thy sight, O Lord, my strength, and my redeemer.

*Psalm 49:3 My mouth shall speak of wisdom; and the meditation of my heart shall be of understanding.

*Psalm 63:6 when I remember thee upon my bed, and meditate on thee in the night watches.

*Psalm 77:12 I will meditate also of all thy work, and talk of thy doings.

*Psalm 104:34 My meditation of him shall be sweet: I will be glad in the Lord.

*Psalm 119:15 I will meditate in thy precepts, and have respect unto thy ways.

*Psalm 119:97 O how love I thy law! it is my meditation all the day.

*Psalm 119:99 I have more understanding than all my teachers: for thy testimonies are my meditation.

*Psalm 143:5 I remember the days of old; I meditate on all thy works; I muse on the work of thy hands.

*1 Timothy 4:15 Meditate upon these things; give thyself wholly to them; that thy profiting may appear to all.

*Psalm 39:3 My heart was hot within me, while I was musing the fire burned: then spake I with my tongue,

Renewing of the Mind

when you give your heart to Jesus Christ, you're born again, washed in the blood, redeemed, a child of God. From this point forward a wonderful transformation will begin to happen as you start renewing your mind with the word of God. The following Scriptures are powerful promises that you should meditate on every day unto the reality of Christ overwhelms all your natural surroundings. As your mind is renewed the new creation will step forth in your life and begin to direct and dominate everything you do and say. Christ will be manifested in you, to you, through you, by you, and for you.

*Romans 12:1 I beseech you therefore, brethren, by the mercies of God, that ye present your bodies a living sacrifice, holy, acceptable unto God, which is your reasonable service. 2 And be not conformed to this world: but be ye transformed by the renewing of your mind, that ye may prove what is that good, and acceptable, and perfect, will of God.

*James 1:21 Wherefore lay apart all filthiness and superfluity of naughtiness, and receive with meekness the engrafted word, which is able to save your souls.

*2 Timothy 3:16 All scripture is given by inspiration of God, and is profitable for doctrine, for reproof, for correction, for instruction in righteousness:17 That the man of God may be perfect, thoroughly furnished unto all good works.

*Psalm 19:7 The law of the Lord is perfect, converting the soul: the testimony of the Lord is sure, making wise the simple.

*Psalm 23:3 He restoreth my soul: he leadeth me in the paths of righteousness for his name's sake.

In Perfect Agreement With God

God is diligently searching for those who will simply be in agreement with him. what happened is that when man partook of sin he was put out of harmony with God. Jesus Christ was one with the Father, in word, deed and action. He boldly declared that if you hear me you hear the Father. The words he spoke he declared were not his but the Fathers. Even the works that he did were not of him but from the Father. The last words we hear Christ pray before he went to the garden of Gethsemane were: *Father make them one with us even as we are one!*

*John 17:21 that they all may be one; as thou, Father, art in me, and I in thee, that they also may be one in us: that the world may believe that thou hast sent me. 22 And the glory which thou gavest me I have given them; that they may be one, even as we are one:

*2 Chronicles 16:9 For the eyes of the Lord run to and fro throughout the whole earth, to shew himself strong in the behalf of them whose heart is perfect toward him.

*1 Peter 3:12 For the eyes of the Lord are over the righteous, and his ears are open unto their prayers: but the face of the Lord is against them that do evil.

*Amos 3:3 Can two walk together, except they be agreed?

*Colossians 3:17 - And whatsoever ye do in word or deed, [do] all in the name of the Lord Jesus, giving thanks to God and the Father by him.

The Power of God's Word

Just this one particular subject alone could be never ending. There are many Scriptures dealing with the importance of the word. There are whole chapters that you and I could memorize and meditate upon, but that would be beyond the scope of this book. I will give to you what I would consider the most powerful Scriptures that are available dealing with God's word. Memorize these Scriptures and meditate upon them daily will surely bring an amazing change in your life in perspective.

*John 1:1 In the beginning was the Word, and the Word was with God, and the Word was God.

*John 1:14 And the Word was made flesh, and dwelt among us, (and we beheld his glory, the glory as of the only begotten of the Father,) full of grace and truth.

*John 6:63 It is the spirit that quickeneth; the flesh profiteth nothing: the words that I speak unto you, they are spirit, and they are life.

*Hebrews 4:12 For the word of God is quick, and powerful, and sharper than any twoedged sword, piercing even to the dividing asunder of soul and spirit, and of the joints and marrow, and is a discerner of the thoughts and intents of the heart.

*Psalm 107:20 He sent his word, and healed them, and delivered them from their destructions.

*Luke 21:33 Heaven and earth shall pass away: but my words shall not pass away.

*Psalm 138:2 I will worship toward thy holy temple, and praise thy name for thy loving kindness and for thy truth: for thou hast magnified thy word above all thy name.

*Isaiah 55:11 so shall my word be that goeth forth out of my mouth: it shall not return unto me void, but it shall accomplish that which I please, and it shall prosper in the thing whereto I sent it.

*Isaiah 40:8 The grass withereth, the flower fadeth: but the word of our God shall stand for ever.

*1 Peter 1:25 But the word of the Lord endureth for ever.

*2 Timothy 3:16 All scripture [is] given by inspiration of God, and [is] profitable for doctrine, for reproof, for correction, for instruction in righteousness:

---

*Jeremiah 23:29 - [Is] not my word like as a fire? saith the LORD; and like a hammer [that] breaketh the rock in pieces?

---

*Psalms 119:105 Thy word [is] a lamp unto my feet, and a light unto my path.

---

*Revelation 12:11 - And they overcame him by the blood of the Lamb, and by the word of their testimony; and they loved not their lives unto the death.

---

*Ephesians 6:17 - And take the helmet of salvation, and the sword of the Spirit, which is the word of God:

---

*2 Corinthians 10:4 - (For the weapons of our warfare [are] not carnal, but mighty through God to the pulling down of strong holds;)

---

*Romans 10:17 - So then faith [cometh] by hearing, and hearing by the word of God.

---

*John 17:17 - Sanctify them through thy truth: thy word is truth.

*Matthew 4:4 - But he answered and said, It is written, Man shall not live by bread alone, but by every word that proceedeth out of the mouth of God.

*1 Peter 1:23 being born again, not of corruptible seed, but of incorruptible, by the word of God, which liveth and abideth for ever.

*1 Peter 2:2 as newborn babes, desire the sincere milk of the word, that ye may grow thereby:

CHAPTER TWO
JESUS CHRIST

The verses in this chapter will seem to be a little bit overwhelming in the beginning, but these Scriptures are an absolute must when it comes to hiding the word of God in your heart. All of our life as a believer is based on the revelation of Jesus Christ. From Matthew chapter 1 to the end of the book of Revelation, Jesus Christ is spoken of in a personal way over 9000 times. It is at the revelation of Jesus Christ in which faith will begin to arise in your heart to accomplish the perfect will of the Father. Without this revelation of who Christ really is, we can accomplish nothing. Go over these Scriptures slowly as you meditate upon them, asking the Holy Spirit to quicken them to you in a profound way, in order to transform you into the likeness and the image of God. In order to become a partaker of all of God's wonderful nature and divine characteristics.

The Reality of Christ

*John 15:5 I am the vine, ye are the branches: He that abideth in me, and I in him, the same bringeth forth much fruit: for without me ye can do nothing.

---

*John 1:1 In the beginning was the Word, and the Word was with God, and the Word was God. 2 The same was in the beginning with God. 3 All things were made by him; and without him was not anything made that was made. 4 In him was life; and the life was the light of men. 5 And the light shineth in darkness; and the darkness comprehended it not.

---

*John 1:14 And the Word was made flesh, and dwelt among us, (and we beheld his glory, the glory as of the only begotten of the Father,) full of grace and truth.

---

*Colossians 2:9 For in him (Christ) dwelleth all the fulness of the Godhead bodily. 10 And ye are complete in him, which is the head of all principality and power:

---

*Hebrews 1:1 God, who at sundry times and in divers manners spake in time past unto the fathers by the prophets, 2 hath in these last days spoken unto us by his Son, whom he hath appointed heir of all things, by whom also he made the worlds; 3 who being the brightness of his glory, and the express image of his person, and upholding all things by the word of his power, when he had by himself purged our sins, sat down on the right hand of the Majesty on high;

*Philippians 2:5 Let this mind be in you, which was also in Christ Jesus: 6 who, being in the form of God, thought it not robbery to be equal with God: 7 but made himself of no reputation, and took upon him the form of a servant, and was made in the likeness of men: 8 and being found in fashion as a man, he humbled himself, and became obedient unto death, even the death of the cross. 9 Wherefore God also hath highly exalted him, and given him a name which is above every name: 10 that at the name of Jesus every knee should bow, of things in heaven, and things in earth, and things under the earth; 11 and that every tongue should confess that Jesus Christ is Lord, to the glory of God the Father.

*Colossians 3:1 If ye then be risen with Christ, seek those things which are above, where Christ sitteth on the right hand of God. 2 Set your affection on things above, not on things on the earth. 3 For ye are dead, and your life is hid with Christ in God. 4 When Christ, who is our life, shall appear, then shall ye also appear with him in glory.

*John 6:53 Then Jesus said unto them, Verily, verily, I say unto you, Except ye eat the flesh of the Son of man, and drink his blood, ye have no life in you. 54 Whoso eateth my flesh, and drinketh my blood, hath eternal life; and I will raise him up at the last day. 55 For my flesh is meat indeed, and my blood is drink indeed. 56 He that eateth my flesh, and drinketh my blood, dwelleth in me, and I in him. 57 As the living Father hath sent me, and I live by the Father: so he that eateth me, even he shall live by me. 58 This is that bread which came down from heaven: not as your fathers did eat manna, and are dead: he that eateth of this bread shall live forever.

---

*1 Timothy 3:16 And without controversy great is the mystery of godliness: God was manifest in the flesh, justified in the Spirit, seen of angels, preached unto the Gentiles, believed on in the world, received up into glory.

---

*Isaiah 9:6 For unto us a child is born, unto us a son is given: and the government shall be upon his shoulder: and his name shall be called Wonderful, Counsellor, The mighty God, The everlasting Father, The Prince of Peace.

---

*Ephesians 1:19 and what is the exceeding greatness of his power to us-ward who believe, according to the working of his mighty power, 20 which he wrought in Christ, when he raised him from the dead, and set him at his own right hand in the heavenly places, 21 far above all principality, and power, and might, and dominion, and every name that is named, not only in this world, but also in that which is to come: 22 and hath put all things under his feet, and gave him to be the head over all things to the church, 23 which is his body, the fulness of him that filleth all in all.

---

*Acts 10:38 how God anointed Jesus of Nazareth with the Holy Ghost and with power: who went about doing good, and healing all that were oppressed of the devil; for God was with him.

---

*Luke 4:18 The Spirit of the Lord is upon me, because he hath anointed me to preach the gospel to the poor; he hath sent me to heal the brokenhearted, to preach deliverance to the captives, and recovering of sight to the blind, to set at liberty them that are bruised, 19 to preach the acceptable year of the Lord.

---

*1 John 3:8 He that committeth sin is of the devil; for the devil sinneth from the beginning. For this purpose the Son of God was manifested, that he might destroy the works of the devil.

---

*Psalm 89:26 He shall cry unto me, Thou art my father, my God, and the rock of my salvation.27 Also I will make him my firstborn, higher than the kings of the earth.28 My mercy will I keep for him for evermore, and my covenant shall stand fast with him.29 His seed also will I make to endure forever, and his throne as the days of heaven.

---

*Hebrews 13:8 Jesus Christ the same yesterday, and today, and forever.

---

*Romans 11:36 For of him, and through him, and to him, are all things: to whom be glory forever. Amen.

---

*1 Peter 3:21........ by the resurrection of Jesus Christ: 22 who is gone into heaven, and is on the right hand of God; angels and authorities and powers being made subject unto him.

---

*Isaiah 49:24 Shall the prey be taken from the mighty, or the lawful captive delivered?:25 But thus saith the Lord, Even the captives of the mighty shall be taken away, and the prey of the terrible shall be delivered: for I will contend with him that contendeth with thee, and I will save thy children.

*Ephesians 4: 8 Wherefore he saith, When he ascended up on high, he led captivity captive, and gave gifts unto men. 9 (Now that he ascended, what is it but that he also descended first into the lower parts of the earth?10 He that descended is the same also that ascended up far above all heavens, that he might fill all things.)

---

*Colossians 1:13 who hath delivered us from the power of darkness, and hath translated us into the kingdom of his dear Son: 14 in whom we have redemption through his blood, even the forgiveness of sins: 15 who is the image of the invisible God, the firstborn of every creature: 16 for by him were all things created, that are in heaven, and that are in earth, visible and invisible, whether they be thrones, or dominions, or principalities, or powers: all things were created by him, and for him: 17 and he is before all things, and by him all things consist. 18 And he is the head of the body, the church: who is the beginning, the firstborn from the dead; that in all things he might have the preeminence. 19 For it pleased the Father that in him should all fulness dwell; 20 and, having made peace through the blood of his cross, by him to reconcile all things unto himself; by him, I say, whether they be things in earth, or things in heaven.

---

*Hebrews 2:8 thou hast put all things in subjection under his feet. For in that he put all in subjection under him, he left nothing that is not put under him. But now we see not yet all things put under him. 9 But we see Jesus, who was made a little lower than the angels for the suffering of death, crowned with glory and honour; that he by the grace of God should taste death for every man.10 For it became him, for whom are all things, and by whom are all things, in bringing many sons unto glory, to make the captain of their salvation perfect through sufferings.

---

*Acts 4:10 be it known unto you all, and to all the people of Israel, that by the name of Jesus Christ of Nazareth, whom ye crucified, whom God raised from the dead, even by him doth this man stand here before you whole. 11 This is the stone which was set at nought of you builders, which is become the head of the corner. 12 Neither is there salvation in any other: for there is none other name under heaven given among men, whereby we must be saved.

*Ephesians 3:14 For this cause I bow my knees unto the Father of our Lord Jesus Christ,15 of whom the whole family in heaven and earth is named, 16 that he would grant you, according to the riches of his glory, to be strengthened with might by his Spirit in the inner man; 17 that Christ may dwell in your hearts by faith; that ye, being rooted and grounded in love, 18 may be able to comprehend with all saints what is the breadth, and length, and depth, and height; 19 and to know the love of Christ, which passeth knowledge, that ye might be filled with all the fulness of God.20 Now unto him that is able to do exceeding abundantly above all that we ask or think, according to the power that worketh in us, 21 unto him be glory in the church by Christ Jesus throughout all ages, world without end. Amen.

*1 Peter 1:8 whom having not seen, ye love; in whom, though now ye see him not, yet believing, ye rejoice with joy unspeakable and full of glory:

In the Name of Jesus

The following scriptures are a declaration of the power and authority that we have in the name of Jesus. There is no other name that has been exalted above all else to bring in the subjection all of the powers and authorities that be. As we submit to Jesus Christ, putting absolute faith and confidence in his name will enter into a wonderful realm of victory. For us to be defeated, God would have to be defeated. Everything we do we do in the name of Jesus Christ of the glory of the Father. Let us feast upon this wonderful name drinking in its beauty, and eating of the substance.

*John 14:13-14 - And whatsoever ye shall ask in my name, that will I do, that the Father may be glorified in the Son.

*John 16:24 - Hitherto have ye asked nothing in my name: ask, and ye shall receive, that your joy may be full.

*John 14:14 - If ye shall ask any thing in my name, I will do [it].

*John 14:13 - And whatsoever ye shall ask in my name, that will I do, that the Father may be glorified in the Son.

*John 15:16 - Ye have not chosen me, but I have chosen you, and ordained you, that ye should go and bring forth fruit, and [that] your fruit should remain: that whatsoever ye shall ask of the Father in my name, he may give it you.

*Matthew 18:20 - For where two or three are gathered together in my name, there am I in the midst of them.

*Romans 8:32 - He that spared not his own Son, but delivered him up for us all, how shall he not with him also freely give us all things?

---

*John 14:6 - Jesus saith unto him, I am the way, the truth, and the life: no man cometh unto the Father, but by me.

---

*John 10:10 - The thief cometh not, but for to steal, and to kill, and to destroy: I am come that they might have life, and that they might have [it] more abundantly.

---

*Proverbs 18:10 - The name of the LORD [is] a strong tower: the righteous runneth into it, and is safe.

---

*Luke 10:17 And the seventy returned again with joy, saying, Lord, even the devils are subject unto us through thy name.

---

*Mark 16:17 And these signs shall follow them that believe; In my name shall they cast out devils; they shall speak with new tongues;

---

*Psalm 44:5 Through thee will we push down our enemies: through thy name will we tread them under that rise up against us.

---

*Psalm 108:13 Through God we shall do valiantly: for he it is that shall tread down our enemies.

---

*Psalm 23

A Psalm of David.

1 The Lord is my shepherd; I shall not want.

2 He maketh me to lie down in green pastures:

he leadeth me beside the still waters.

3 He restoreth my soul:

he leadeth me in the paths of righteousness for his name's sake.

4 Yea, though I walk through the valley of the shadow of death,

I will fear no evil: for thou art with me;

thy rod and thy staff they comfort me.

5 Thou preparest a table before me in the presence of mine enemies:

thou anointest my head with oil; my cup runneth over.

6 Surely goodness and mercy shall follow me all the days of my life:

and I will dwell in the house of the Lord for ever.

CHAPTER THREE
The Divine Nature

The whole purpose of Christ coming was in order to bring change to our nature. When you invite Christ into your heart, the incorruptible seed of the word of life is implanted within the soil of your being. As you meditate upon the truths of this amazing plan the fruits of the spirit will begin to be manifested in your attitude, character and nature. We must meditate upon the Scriptures in order for the Holy Spirit has that which is necessary to bring to pass the perfect will of the father with in our personalities and character. The Scripture very boldly declares that we are the sons of God, and it does not yet appear what we shall be. That natural eyes have not seen nor ears heard, neither entered into the heart of man what God has planned for them that love him.

*1 John 3:1 Behold, what manner of love the Father hath bestowed upon us, that we should be called the sons of God: therefore the world knoweth us not, because it knew him not. 2 Beloved, now are we the sons of God, and it doth not yet appear what we shall be: but we know that, when he shall appear, we shall be like him; for we shall see him as he is. 3 And every man that hath this hope in him purifieth himself, even as he is pure.

*2 Corinthians 5:17 Therefore if any man be in Christ, he is a new creature: old things are passed away; behold, all things are become new.

*Ezekiel 36:26 A new heart also will I give you, and a new spirit will I put within you: and I will take away the stony heart out of your flesh, and I will give you an heart of flesh.

*John 3:3 Jesus answered and said unto him, Verily, verily, I say unto thee, Except a man be born again, he cannot see the kingdom of God.

*Ephesians 4:22 That ye put off concerning the former conversation the old man, which is corrupt according to the deceitful lusts;23 And be renewed in the spirit of your mind;24 And that ye put on the new man, which after God is created in righteousness and true holiness.

*2 Corinthians 5:21 For he hath made him to be sin for us, who knew no sin; that we might be made the righteousness of God in him.

*Romans 6:5 For if we have been planted together in the likeness of his death, we shall be also in the likeness of his resurrection:

*2 Corinthians 6:…….as God hath said, I will dwell in them, and walk in them; and I will be their God, and they shall be my people.

*2 Corinthians 3:18 But we all, with open face beholding as in a glass the glory of the Lord, are changed into the same image from glory to glory, even as by the Spirit of the Lord.

*2 Peter 1:4 Whereby are given unto us exceeding great and precious promises: that by these ye might be partakers of the divine nature, having escaped the corruption that is in the world through lust.

*Romans 8:18 For I reckon that the sufferings of this present time are not worthy to be compared with the glory which shall be revealed in us.

*Romans 8:14 For as many as are led by the Spirit of God, they are the sons of God.15 For ye have not received the spirit of bondage again to fear; but ye have received the Spirit of adoption, whereby we cry, Abba, Father.

*Galatians 4:6 And because ye are sons, God hath sent forth the Spirit of his Son into your hearts, crying, Abba, Father.

*1 John 4:4 Ye are of God, little children, and have overcome them: because greater is he that is in you, than he that is in the world.

Walking in the Spirit

In order to walk in the spirit we must be full of the word of God. The divine influence of the Holy Spirit must have complete possession of our lives. There are many scriptures that deal with his particular subject of living , moving, operating, and flowing in the Holy Ghost. God is looking for those who will be completely yielded and surrendered to him in all areas of their life. when we walk in the spirit we will not fulfill the lust of the flesh. Meditate upon these realities and you will soon begin to see wonderful and amazing transformation in all that you do and say. When you walk in the spirit the fruits of the spirit will be manifested in your life.

*Galatians 5:16 This I say then, Walk in the Spirit, and ye shall not fulfil the lust of the flesh. 17 For the flesh lusteth against the Spirit, and the Spirit against the flesh: and these are contrary the one to the other: so that ye cannot do the things that ye would.

---

*Galatians 5:24 And they that are Christ's have crucified the flesh with the affections and lusts. 25 If we live in the Spirit, let us also walk in the Spirit. 26 Let us not be desirous of vain glory, provoking one another, envying one another.

---

*1 Peter 2:11 Dearly beloved, I beseech you as strangers and pilgrims, abstain from fleshly lusts, which war against the soul;

---

*Romans 8:12 Therefore, brethren, we are debtors, not to the flesh, to live after the flesh.13 For if ye live after the flesh, ye shall die: but if ye through the Spirit do mortify the deeds of the body, ye shall live.14 For as many as are led by the Spirit of God, they are the sons of God.

---

*Colossians 3:9 Lie not one to another, seeing that ye have put off the old man with his deeds;10 And have put on the new man, which is renewed in knowledge after the image of him that created him:

---

*Deuteronomy8:6 Therefore thou shalt keep the commandments of the Lord thy God, to walk in his ways, and to fear him.

*Romans 8:1 There is therefore now no condemnation to them which are in Christ Jesus, who walk not after the flesh, but after the Spirit. 2 For the law of the Spirit of life in Christ Jesus hath made me free from the law of sin and death. 3 For what the law could not do, in that it was weak through the flesh, God sending his own Son in the likeness of sinful flesh, and for sin, condemned sin in the flesh:

*Colossians 1:10 that ye might walk worthy of the Lord unto all pleasing, being fruitful in every good work, and increasing in the knowledge of God;

*1 Thessalonians 2:12 that ye would walk worthy of God, who hath called you unto his kingdom and glory.

*2 Corinthians 5:7 (for we walk by faith, not by sight)

Romans 1:17 For therein is the righteousness of God revealed from faith to faith: as it is written, The just shall live by faith.

*Galatians 2:20 I am crucified with Christ: nevertheless I live; yet not I, but Christ liveth in me: and the life which I now live in the flesh I live by the faith of the Son of God, who loved me, and gave himself for me.

*Galatians 3:11 But that no man is justified by the law in the sight of God, it is evident: for, The just shall live by faith.

*Hebrews 10:38 Now the just shall live by faith: but if any man draw back, my soul shall have no pleasure in him.

---

*John 8:12 Then spake Jesus again unto them, saying, I am the light of the world: he that followeth me shall not walk in darkness, but shall have the light of life.

---

*Ephesians 5:8 For ye were sometimes darkness, but now are ye light in the Lord: walk as children of light:

---

*1 John 1:7 But if we walk in the light, as he is in the light, we have fellowship one with another, and the blood of Jesus Christ his Son cleanseth us from all sin.

Fruits of the Spirit

*Galatians 5:22 But the fruit of the Spirit is love, joy, peace, longsuffering, gentleness, goodness, faith, 23 meekness, temperance: against such there is no law.

---

*Colossians 3:12 Put on therefore, as the elect of God, holy and beloved, bowels of mercies, kindness, humbleness of mind, meekness, longsuffering;13 Forbearing one another, and forgiving one another, if any man have a quarrel against any: even as Christ forgave you, so also do ye.14 And above all these things put on charity, which is the bond of perfectness.15 And let the peace of God rule in your hearts, to the which also ye are called in one body; and be ye thankful.

---

*Ephesians 5:9 (For the fruit of the Spirit is in all goodness and righteousness and truth;)

*John 15:2 Every branch in me that beareth not fruit he taketh away: and every branch that beareth fruit, he purgeth it, that it may bring forth more fruit.

*James 3:17 But the wisdom that is from above is first pure, then peaceable, gentle, and easy to be intreated, full of mercy and good fruits, without partiality, and without hypocrisy.18 And the fruit of righteousness is sown in peace of them that make peace.

*Philippians 4:4 Rejoice in the Lord always: and again I say, Rejoice.5 Let your moderation be known unto all men. The Lord is at hand.6 Be careful for nothing; but in every thing by prayer and supplication with thanksgiving let your requests be made known unto God.7 And the peace of God, which passeth all understanding, shall keep your hearts and minds through Christ Jesus.

*John 15:16 Ye have not chosen me, but I have chosen you, and ordained you, that ye should go and bring forth fruit, and that your fruit should remain: that whatsoever ye shall ask of the Father in my name, he may give it you.

*2 Peter 1:5 And beside this, giving all diligence, add to your faith virtue; and to virtue knowledge;6 And to knowledge temperance; and to temperance patience; and to patience godliness;7 And to godliness brotherly kindness; and to brotherly kindness charity.8 For if these things be in you, and abound, they make you that ye shall neither be barren nor unfruitful in the knowledge of our Lord Jesus Christ.

*Colossians 1:10 That ye might walk worthy of the Lord unto all pleasing, being fruitful in every good work, and increasing in the knowledge of God;

LOVE

*1 Corinthians 13:4 Love suffereth long, and is kind; Love envieth not; Love vaunteth not itself, is not puffed up,5 Doth not behave itself unseemly, seeketh not her own, is not easily provoked, thinketh no evil;6 Rejoiceth not in iniquity, but rejoiceth in the truth;7 Love Beareth all things, believeth all things, hopeth all things, endureth all things.

---

*1 John 4:7 Beloved, let us love one another: for love is of God; and every one that loveth is born of God, and knoweth God.8 He that loveth not knoweth not God; for God is love.

---

*1 Corinthians 13:13 And now abideth faith, hope, charity, these three; but the greatest of these is charity.

---

*1 John 4:8 - He that loveth not knoweth not God; for God is love.

---

*John 13:34A new commandment I give unto you, That ye love one another; as I have loved you, that ye also love one another.

---

*Romans 5:8 - But God commendeth his love toward us, in that, while we were yet sinners, Christ died for us.

---

*John 3:16 - For God so loved the world, that he gave his only begotten Son, that whosoever believeth in him should not perish, but have everlasting life.

---

*1 John 4:18 - There is no fear in love; but perfect love casteth out fear: because fear hath torment. He that feareth is not made perfect in love.

---

*John 15:13 - Greater love hath no man than this, that a man lay down his life for his friends.

---

*1 John 4:10 - Herein is love, not that we loved God, but that he loved us, and sent his Son [to be] the propitiation for our sins.

---

*John 14:21 - He that hath my commandments, and keepeth them, he it is that loveth me: and he that loveth me shall be loved of my Father, and I will love him, and will manifest myself to him.

---

*Luke 10:27 - And he answering said, Thou shalt love the Lord thy God with all thy heart, and with all thy soul, and with all thy strength, and with all thy mind; and thy neighbour as thyself.

---

*1 John 4:20-21 - If a man say, I love God, and hateth his brother, he is a liar: for he that loveth not his brother whom he hath seen, how can he love God whom he hath not seen?

---

*1 John 4:7 - Beloved, let us love one another: for love is of God; and every one that loveth is born of God, and knoweth God.

*John 14:15 - If ye love me, keep my commandments.

*Colossians 3:14 - And above all these things [put on] charity, which is the bond of perfectness.

*1 John 5:3 For this is the love of God, that we keep his commandments: and his commandments are not grievous.

Joy

*Romans 12:15 Rejoice with them that do rejoice, and weep with them that weep.

*Romans 12:12 - Rejoicing in hope; patient in tribulation; continuing instant in prayer;

*James 1:2 - My brethren, count it all joy when ye fall into divers temptations;

*Philippians 4:4 - Rejoice in the Lord alway: [and] again I say, Rejoice.

*1 Peter 1:8 - Whom having not seen, ye love; in whom, though now ye see [him] not, yet believing, ye rejoice with joy unspeakable and full of glory:

*John 16:24 - Hitherto have ye asked nothing in my name: ask, and ye shall receive, that your joy may be full.

*Romans 15:13 - Now the God of hope fill you with all joy and peace in believing, that ye may abound in hope, through the power of the Holy Ghost.

*Romans 14:17 - For the kingdom of God is not meat and drink; but righteousness, and peace, and joy in the Holy Ghost.

*1 Thessalonians 5:16 - Rejoice evermore.

*2 Corinthians 8:2 - How that in a great trial of affliction the abundance of their joy and their deep poverty abounded unto the riches of their liberality.

*Romans 5:11 - And not only [so], but we also joy in God through our Lord Jesus Christ, by whom we have now received the atonement.

*1 Peter 4:13 - But rejoice, inasmuch as ye are partakers of Christ's sufferings; that, when his glory shall be revealed, ye may be glad also with exceeding joy.

*Luke 15:10 - Likewise, I say unto you, there is joy in the presence of the angels of God over one sinner that repenteth.

*James 1:2-4 - My brethren, count it all joy when ye fall into divers temptations;

*Colossians 1:11 - Strengthened with all might, according to his glorious power, unto all patience and longsuffering with joyfulness;

*Psalms 4:7 - Thou hast put gladness in my heart, more than in the time [that] their corn and their wine increased.

*1 John 1:4 - And these things write we unto you, that your joy may be full.

*Jeremiah 29:11 - For I know the thoughts that I think toward you, saith the LORD, thoughts of peace, and not of evil, to give you an expected end.

*Isaiah 55:12 - For ye shall go out with joy, and be led forth with peace: the mountains and the hills shall break forth before you into singing, and all the trees of the field shall clap [their] hands.

*Psalms 100:1 Make a joyful noise unto the LORD, all ye lands.

*Proverbs 17:22 - A merry heart doeth good [like] a medicine: but a broken spirit drieth the bones.

*Philippians 3:3 - For we are the circumcision, which worship God in the spirit, and rejoice in Christ Jesus, and have no confidence in the flesh.

*Psalms 70:4 - Let all those that seek thee rejoice and be glad in thee: and let such as love thy salvation say continually, Let God be magnified.

*Psalms 126:5 - They that sow in tears shall reap in joy.

*Ephesians 5:18 - And be not drunk with wine, wherein is excess; but be filled with the Spirit;

*Psalms 104:34 - My meditation of him shall be sweet: I will be glad in the LORD.

*Psalms 100:2 - Serve the LORD with gladness: come before his presence with singing.

*Psalms 64:10 - The righteous shall be glad in the LORD, and shall trust in him; and all the upright in heart shall glory.

*Psalms 30:11 - Thou hast turned for me my mourning into dancing: thou hast put off my sackcloth, and girded me with gladness;

*Psalms 19:8 - The statutes of the LORD [are] right, rejoicing the heart: the commandment of the LORD [is] pure, enlightening the eyes.

*Psalms 16:11 - Thou wilt shew me the path of life: in thy presence [is] fulness of joy; at thy right hand [there are] pleasures for evermore.

*Psalms 5:11 - But let all those that put their trust in thee rejoice: let them ever shout for joy, because thou defendest them: let them also that love thy name be joyful in thee.

*1 Thessalonians 2:19 - For what [is] our hope, or joy, or crown of rejoicing? [Are] not even ye in the presence of our Lord Jesus Christ at his coming?

---

*Jeremiah 15:16 - Thy words were found, and I did eat them; and thy word was unto me the joy and rejoicing of mine heart: for I am called by thy name, **O LORD** God of hosts.

CHAPTER FOUR
CONTINUED FRUITS

Peace

*Matthew 5:9 - Blessed [are] the peacemakers: for they shall be called the children of God.

---

*Philippians 4:7 - And the peace of God, which passeth all understanding, shall keep your hearts and minds through Christ Jesus.

---

*2 Thessalonians 3:16 - Now the Lord of peace himself give you peace always by all means. The Lord [be] with you all.

---

*John 14:27 - Peace I leave with you, my peace I give unto you: not as the world giveth, give I unto you. Let not your heart be troubled, neither let it be afraid.

---

*1 Peter 3:11 - Let him eschew evil, and do good; let him seek peace, and ensue it.

---

*1 Peter 5:7 - Casting all your care upon him; for he careth for you.

*Isaiah 26:3 - Thou wilt keep [him] in perfect peace, [whose] mind [is] stayed [on thee]: because he trusteth in thee.

---

*John 16:33 - These things I have spoken unto you, that in me ye might have peace. In the world ye shall have tribulation: but be of good cheer; I have overcome the world.

---

*Hebrews 12:14 - Follow peace with all [men], and holiness, without which no man shall see the Lord:

---

*Philippians 4:9 - Those things, which ye have both learned, and received, and heard, and seen in me, do: and the God of peace shall be with you.

---

*Isaiah 12:2 - Behold, God [is] my salvation; I will trust, and not be afraid: for the LORD JEHOVAH [is] my strength and [my] song; he also is become my salvation.

---

*Romans 8:6 - For to be carnally minded [is] death; but to be spiritually minded [is] life and peace.

---

*Colossians 3:15 - And let the peace of God rule in your hearts, to the which also ye are called in one body; and be ye thankful.

*James 3:18 - And the fruit of righteousness is sown in peace of them that make peace.

---

*Romans 14:19 - Let us therefore follow after the things which make for peace, and things wherewith one may edify another.

---

*Psalms 37:4 - Delight thyself also in the LORD; and he shall give thee the desires of thine heart.

---

*Isaiah 32:17 - And the work of righteousness shall be peace; and the effect of righteousness quietness and assurance for ever.

---

*Proverbs 3:24 - When thou liest down, thou shalt not be afraid: yea, thou shalt lie down, and thy sleep shall be sweet.

---

*John 7:38 - He that believeth on me, as the scripture hath said, out of his belly shall flow rivers of living water.

---

*Isaiah 54:13 - And all thy children [shall be] taught of the LORD; and great [shall be] the peace of thy children.

---

*Psalms 34:14 - Depart from evil, and do good; seek peace, and pursue it.

*1 Peter 3:10 - For he that will love life, and see good days, let him refrain his tongue from evil, and his lips that they speak no guile:

*Jeremiah 33:6 - Behold, I will bring it health and cure, and I will cure them, and will reveal unto them the abundance of peace and truth.

*Isaiah 55:12 - For ye shall go out with joy, and be led forth with peace: the mountains and the hills shall break forth before you into singing, and all the trees of the field shall clap [their] hands.

Longsuffering

*Ephesians 4:2 - With all lowliness and meekness, with longsuffering, forbearing one another in love;

*2 Peter 3:9 - The Lord is not slack concerning his promise, as some men count slackness; but is longsuffering to us-ward, not willing that any should perish, but that all should come to repentance.

*Romans 8:28 - And we know that all things work together for good to them that love God, to them who are the called according to [his] purpose.

*James 4:7 - Submit yourselves therefore to God. Resist the devil, and he will flee from you.

*Ezekiel 18:20 - The soul that sinneth, it shall die. The son shall not bear the iniquity of the father, neither shall the father bear the iniquity of the son.

*Ezekiel 18:4 - Behold, all souls are mine; as the soul of the father, so also the soul of the son is mine: the soul that sinneth, it shall die.

*Exodus 34:6 - And the LORD passed by before him, and proclaimed, The LORD, The LORD God, merciful and gracious, longsuffering, and abundant in goodness and truth,

*Romans 2:4 - Or despisest thou the riches of his goodness and forbearance and longsuffering; not knowing that the goodness of God leadeth thee to repentance?

Gentleness

*Psalms 18:35 - Thou hast also given me the shield of thy salvation: and thy right hand hath holden me up, and thy gentleness hath made me great.

*2 Timothy 2:24-26 - And the servant of the Lord must not strive; but be gentle unto all [men], apt to teach, patient,   (Read More...)

---

*James 1:19-20 - Wherefore, my beloved brethren, let every man be swift to hear, slow to speak, slow to wrath: (Read More...)

---

*Isaiah 40:11 - He shall feed his flock like a shepherd: he shall gather the lambs with his arm, and carry [them] in his bosom, [and] shall gently lead those that are with young.

---

*Colossians 3:12 - Put on therefore, as the elect of God, holy and beloved, bowels of mercies, kindness, humbleness of mind, meekness, longsuffering;

---

*Proverbs 15:1 - A soft answer turneth away wrath: but grievous words stir up anger.

---

*Micah 6:8 - He hath shewed thee, O man, what [is] good; and what doth the LORD require of thee, but to do justly, and to love mercy, and to walk humbly with thy God?

---

*John 14:6 - Jesus saith unto him, I am the way, the truth, and the life: no man cometh unto the Father, but by me.

*Matthew 6:19-21 - Lay not up for yourselves treasures upon earth, where moth and rust doth corrupt, and where thieves break through and steal: (Read More...)

*Isaiah 53:7 - He was oppressed, and he was afflicted, yet he opened not his mouth: he is brought as a lamb to the slaughter, and as a sheep before her shearers is dumb, so he openeth not his mouth.

*Hebrews 13:5 - [Let your] conversation [be] without covetousness; [and be] content with such things as ye have: for he hath said, I will never leave thee, nor forsake thee.

*1 Peter 2:23 - Who, when he was reviled, reviled not again; when he suffered, he threatened not; but committed [himself] to him that judgeth righteously:

*1 Timothy 6:11 - But thou, O man of God, flee these things; and follow after righteousness, godliness, faith, love, patience, meekness.

Goodness

*Romans 8:28 - And we know that all things work together for good to them that love God, to them who are the called according to [his] purpose.

*Psalms 31:19 - [Oh] how great [is] thy goodness, which thou hast laid up for them that fear thee; [which] thou hast wrought for them that trust in thee before the sons of men!

*Psalms 23:6 - Surely goodness and mercy shall follow me all the days of my life: and I will dwell in the house of the LORD for ever.

*Romans 12:9 ..... Abhor that which is evil; cleave to that which is good.

Faithfulness

*Proverbs 28:20 - A faithful man shall abound with blessings: but he that maketh haste to be rich shall not be innocent.

*Luke 16:10-12 - He that is faithful in that which is least is faithful also in much: and he that is unjust in the least is unjust also in much.

*John 14:15 - If ye love me, keep my commandments.

*Jeremiah 1:5 - Before I formed thee in the belly I knew thee; and before thou camest forth out of the womb I sanctified thee, [and] I ordained thee a prophet unto the nations.

*1 Corinthians 10:13 - There hath no temptation taken you but such as is common to man: but God [is] faithful, who will not suffer you to be tempted above that ye are able; but will with the temptation also make a way to escape, that ye may be able to bear [it].

---

*Matthew 10:22 - And ye shall be hated of all [men] for my name's sake: but he that endureth to the end shall be saved.

---

*Psalms 91:4 - He shall cover thee with his feathers, and under his wings shalt thou trust: his truth [shall be thy] shield and buckler.

*2 Peter 3:9 - The Lord is not slack concerning his promise, as some men count slackness; but is longsuffering to us-ward, not willing that any should perish, but that all should come to repentance.

---

*1 Timothy 5:8 - But if any provide not for his own, and especially for those of his own house hold.

---

*Romans 10:9 - That if thou shalt confess with thy mouth the Lord Jesus, and shalt believe in thine heart that God hath raised him from the dead, thou shalt be saved.

---

*Proverbs 25:19 Confidence in an unfaithful man in time of trouble is like a broken tooth, and a foot out of joint.

Meekness

*Matthew 5:5 - Blessed [are] the meek: for they shall inherit the earth.

---

*Matthew 11:29 - Take my yoke upon you, and learn of me; for I am meek and lowly in heart: and ye shall find rest unto your souls.

---

*Psalms 25:9 - The meek will he guide in judgment: and the meek will he teach his way.

---

*1 Peter 3:4 - But [let it be] the hidden man of the heart, in that which is not corruptible, [even the ornament] of a meek and quiet spirit, which is in the sight of God of great price.

---

*Psalms 37:11 - But the meek shall inherit the earth; and shall delight themselves in the abundance of peace.

---

*James 3:13 - Who [is] a wise man and endued with knowledge among you? let him shew out of a good conversation his works with meekness of wisdom.

---

*Numbers 12:3 - (Now the man Moses [was] very meek, above all the men which [were] upon the face of the earth.)

---

*James 1:21 - Wherefore lay apart all filthiness and superfluity of naughtiness, and receive with meekness the engrafted word, which is able to save your souls.

---

*Galatians 6:1 - Brethren, if a man be overtaken in a fault, ye which are spiritual, restore such an one in the spirit of meekness; considering thyself, lest thou also be tempted.

---

*Ephesians 4:2 - With all lowliness and meekness, with longsuffering, forbearing one another in love;

---

*1 Peter 5:7 - Casting all your care upon him; for he careth for you.

---

*2 Timothy 2:25 - In meekness instructing those that oppose themselves; if God peradventure will give them repentance to the acknowledging of the truth;

---

*1 Timothy 6:11 - But thou, O man of God, flee these things; and follow after righteousness, godliness, faith, love, patience, meekness.

---

*Psalms 22:26 - The meek shall eat and be satisfied: they shall praise the LORD that seek him: your heart shall live for ever.

*Romans 12:18 - If it be possible, as much as lieth in you, live peaceably with all men.

*Matthew 16:24 - Then said Jesus unto his disciples, If any [man] will come after me, let him deny himself, and take up his cross, and follow me.

*Matthew 5:9 - Blessed [are] the peacemakers: for they shall be called the children of God.

Temperance

*1 Corinthians 9:27 - But I keep under my body, and bring [it] into subjection: lest that by any means, when I have preached to others, I myself should be a castaway.

   *Romans 13:14 - But put ye on the Lord Jesus Christ, and make not provision for the flesh, to [fulfil] the lusts [thereof].

   *2 Peter 1:6 - And to knowledge temperance; and to temperance patience; and to patience godliness;

*1 Peter 5:8 - Be sober, be vigilant; because your adversary the devil, as a roaring lion, walketh about, seeking whom he may devour:

*1 Thessalonians 5:21 - Prove all things; hold fast that which is good.

*Galatians 6:7-8 - Be not deceived; God is not mocked: for whatsoever a man soweth, that shall he also reap.   (Read More...)

*Romans 8:37 - Nay, in all these things we are more than conquerors through him that loved us.

*John 11:25 - Jesus said unto her, I am the resurrection, and the life: he that believeth in me, though he were dead, yet shall he live:

*Philippians 4:13 - I can do all things through Christ which strengtheneth me.

*2 Corinthians 5:21 - For he hath made him [to be] sin for us, who knew no sin; that we might be made the righteousness of God in him.

*Romans 3:23 - For all have sinned, and come short of the glory of God;

---

*John 8:32 - And ye shall know the truth, and the truth shall make you free.

---

*John 14:6 - Jesus saith unto him, I am the way, the truth, and the life: no man cometh unto the Father, but by me.

CHAPTER FIVE
HEALING

    Healing is such an important part of God's redemptive plan for men. There's many Scriptures that are given to us in the old and the new pertaining to this particular subject. As you hide the word of God in your heart through meditation may the Scriptures become alive inside of you. May the Lord grant unto you a revelation of the price that was paid for your physical, mental, and emotional healing. For 40 years I have fought the fight of faith when it comes to divine healing for myself and many others. Christ has paid the ultimate price for my physical healing, and I will not allow the enemy to rob me of it. I hope you will be of the same mindset.

    *Isa 53:4-5 Surely he hath borne our griefs, and carried our sorrows: yet we did esteem him stricken, smitten of God, and afflicted….But he was wounded for our transgressions, he was bruised for our iniquities: the chastisement of our peace was upon him; and with his stripes we are healed.

---

    *Prov 4:20-22 My son, attend to my words; incline thine ear unto my sayings….Let them not depart from thine eyes; keep them in the midst of thine heart….For they are life unto those that find them, and health to all their flesh.

---

    *3 John 1:2 Beloved, I wish above all things that thou mayest prosper and be in health, even as thy soul prospereth.

---

    *1 John 5:14-15 And this is the confidence that we have in him, that, if we ask any thing according to his will, he heareth us:…And if we know that he hear us, whatsoever we ask, we know that we have the petitions that we desired of him.

---

*James 1:17 Every good gift and every perfect gift is from above, and cometh down from the Father of lights, with whom is no variableness, neither shadow of turning.

---

*Mal 3:6 For I am the LORD, I change not; therefore ye sons of Jacob are not consumed.

---

*Isa 41:10 Fear thou not; for I am with thee: be not dismayed; for I am thy God: I will strengthen thee; yea, I will help thee; yea, I will uphold thee with the right hand of my righteousness.

---

*Deut 7:15 And the LORD will take away from thee all sickness, and will put none of the evil diseases of Egypt, which thou knowest, upon thee; but will lay them upon all them that hate thee.

---

*Exo 15:26 And said, If thou wilt diligently hearken to the voice of the LORD thy God, and wilt do that which is right in his sight, and wilt give ear to his commandments, and keep all his statutes, I will put none of these diseases upon thee, which I have brought upon the Egyptians: for I am the LORD that healeth thee.

---

*Jer 30:17 For I will restore health unto thee, and I will heal thee of thy wounds, saith the LORD;

---

*Jer 33:6 Behold, I will bring it health and cure, and I will cure them, and will reveal unto them the abundance of peace and truth.

---

*Deut 30:19-20 I call heaven and earth to record this day against you, that I have set before you life and death, blessing and cursing: therefore choose life, that both thou and thy seed may live:…That thou mayest love the LORD thy God, and that thou mayest obey his voice, and that thou mayest cleave unto him: for he is thy life, and the length of thy days: that thou mayest dwell in the land which the LORD sware unto thy fathers, to Abraham, to Isaac, and to Jacob, to give them.

---

*Isa 58:8 Then shall thy light break forth as the morning, and thine health shall spring forth speedily: and thy righteousness shall go before thee; the glory of the LORD shall be thy rereward.

---

*2 Chr 30:20 And the LORD hearkened to Hezekiah, and healed the people.

---

*Num 23:19 God is not a man, that he should lie; neither the son of man, that he should repent: hath he said, and shall he not do it? or hath he spoken, and shall he not make it good?

---

*Psa 105:37 He brought them forth also with silver and gold: and there was not one feeble person among their tribes.

*Psa 103:3 Who forgiveth all thine iniquities; who healeth all thy diseases;

*Psa 147:3 He healeth the broken in heart, and bindeth up their wounds.

*Psa 30:2 O LORD my God, I cried unto thee, and thou hast healed me.

*Psa 34:19 Many are the afflictions of the righteous: but the LORD delivereth him out of them all.

*Psa 42:11 Why art thou cast down, O my soul? and why art thou disquieted within me? hope thou in God: for I shall yet praise him, who is the health of my countenance, and my God.

*Mat 8:17 That it might be fulfilled which was spoken by Esaias the prophet, saying, Himself took our infirmities, and bare our sicknesses.

*1 Pet 2:24 Who his own self bare our sins in his own body on the tree, that we, being dead to sins, should live unto righteousness: by whose stripes ye were healed.

*Gal 3:13,14, Christ hath redeemed us from the curse of the law, being made a curse for us: for it is written, Cursed is every one that hangeth on a tree:...

*Prov 3:1-2 My son, forget not my law; but let thine heart keep my commandments:...For length of days, and long life, and peace, shall they add to thee.

*Mat 4:23-24 And Jesus went about all Galilee, teaching in their synagogues, and preaching the gospel of the kingdom, and healing all manner of sickness and all manner of disease among the people....And his fame went throughout all Syria: and they brought unto him all sick people that were taken with divers diseases and torments, and those which were possessed with devils, and those which were lunatic, and those that had the palsy; and he healed them.

*Mat 12:15 But when Jesus knew it, he withdrew himself from thence: and great multitudes followed him, and he healed them all;

*John 10:10 The thief cometh not, but for to steal, and to kill, and to destroy: I am come that they might have life, and that they might have it more abundantly.

*Acts 10:38 How God anointed Jesus of Nazareth with the Holy Ghost and with power: who went about doing good, and healing all that were oppressed of the devil; for God was with him.

---

*1 John 3:8 He that committeth sin is of the devil; for the devil sinneth from the beginning. For this purpose the Son of God was manifested, that he might destroy the works of the devil.

---

*Mat 10:1 And when he had called unto him his twelve disciples, he gave them power against unclean spirits, to cast them out, and to heal all manner of sickness and all manner of disease.

---

*John 14:12-15 Verily, verily, I say unto you, He that believeth on me, the works that I do shall he do also; and greater works than these shall he do; because I go unto my Father….And whatsoever ye shall ask in my name, that will I do, that the Father may be glorified in the Son….If ye shall ask any thing in my name, I will do it….If ye love me, keep my commandments.

---

*James 5:14-16 Is any sick among you? let him call for the elders of the church; and let them pray over him, anointing him with oil in the name of the Lord:…And the prayer of faith shall save the sick, and the Lord shall raise him up; and if he have committed sins, they shall be forgiven him….Confess your faults one to another, and pray one for another, that ye may be healed. The effectual fervent prayer of a righteous man availeth much.

---

*Mal 4:2 But unto you that fear my name shall the Sun of righteousness arise with healing in his wings; and ye shall go forth, and grow up as calves of the stall.

---

*Psa 107:20 He sent his word, and healed them, and delivered them from their destructions.

---

*Isa 55:11 So shall my word be that goeth forth out of my mouth: it shall not return unto me void, but it shall accomplish that which I please, and it shall prosper in the thing whereto I sent it.

---

*Luke 4: 18 The Spirit of the Lord is upon me, because he hath anointed me to preach the gospel to the poor; he hath sent me to heal the brokenhearted, to preach deliverance to the captives, and recovering of sight to the blind, to set at liberty them that are bruised, 19 to preach the acceptable year of the Lord.

PRAYER

*Philippians 4:6 - Be careful for nothing; but in every thing by prayer and supplication with thanksgiving let your requests be made known unto God.

---

*1 Thessalonians 5:17 - **Pray without ceasing.**

---

*Mark 11:24 - Therefore I say unto you, What things soever ye desire, when ye pray, believe that ye receive [them], and ye shall have [them].

*Ephesians 6:18 - Praying always with all prayer and supplication in the Spirit, and watching thereunto with all perseverance and supplication for all saints;

*James 5:16 - Confess [your] faults one to another, and pray one for another, that ye may be healed. The effectual fervent prayer of a righteous man availeth much.

*Romans 8:26 - Likewise the Spirit also helpeth our infirmities: for we know not what we should pray for as we ought: but the Spirit itself maketh intercession for us with groanings which cannot be uttered.

*Matthew 21:22 - And all things, whatsoever ye shall ask in prayer, believing, ye shall receive.

*1 John 5:14-15 - And this is the confidence that we have in him, that, if we ask any thing according to his will, he heareth us:

*Colossians 4:2 - Continue in prayer, and watch in the same with thanksgiving;

*Psalms 55:17 - Evening, and morning, and at noon, will I pray, and cry aloud: and he shall hear my voice.

*Matthew 18:19 - Again I say unto you, That if two of you shall agree on earth as touching anything that they shall ask, it shall be done for them of my Father which is in heaven.

*Hebrews 4:16 - Let us therefore come boldly unto the throne of grace, that we may obtain mercy, and find grace to help in time of need.

*Matthew 26:39 - And he went a little further, and fell on his face, and prayed, saying, O my Father, if it be possible, let this cup pass from me: nevertheless not as I will, but as thou [wilt].

*Isaiah 55:6 - Seek ye the LORD while he may be found, call ye upon him while he is near:

*2 Chronicles 7:14 - If my people, which are called by my name, shall humble themselves, and pray, and seek my face, and turn from their wicked ways; then will I hear from heaven, and will forgive their sin, and will heal their land.

*Matthew 7:7 - Ask, and it shall be given you; seek, and ye shall find; knock, and it shall be opened unto you:

---

*Psalms 55:16 - As for me, I will call upon God; and the LORD shall save me.

---

*1 Timothy 2:8 - I will therefore that men pray every where, lifting up holy hands, without wrath and doubting.

---

*1 Thessalonians 5:18 - In every thing give thanks: for this is the will of God in Christ Jesus concerning you.

---

*James 4:8 - Draw nigh to God, and he will draw nigh to you. Cleanse [your] hands, [ye] sinners; and purify [your] hearts, [ye] double minded.

---

*John 16:24 - Hitherto have ye asked nothing in my name: ask, and ye shall receive, that your joy may be full.

---

*James 5:17 - Elias was a man subject to like passions as we are, and he prayed earnestly that it might not rain: and it rained not on the earth by the space of three years and six months.

---

*Romans 8:26-27 - Likewise the Spirit also helpeth our infirmities: for we know not what we should pray for as we ought: but the Spirit itself maketh intercession for us with groanings which cannot be uttered.   (Read More...)

---

*Hebrews 11:6 - But without faith [it is] impossible to please [him]: for he that cometh to God must believe that he is, and [that] he is a rewarder of them that diligently seek him.

---

*John 16:23 - And in that day ye shall ask me nothing. Verily, verily, I say unto you, Whatsoever ye shall ask the Father in my name, he will give [it] you.

---

*Romans 10:13 - For whosoever shall call upon the name of the Lord shall be saved.

---

*John 15:16 - Ye have not chosen me, but I have chosen you, and ordained you, that ye should go and bring forth fruit, and [that] your fruit should remain: that whatsoever ye shall ask of the Father in my name, he may give it you.

---

*Jude 1:20 - But ye, beloved, building up yourselves on your most holy faith, praying in the Holy Ghost,

CHAPTER SIX
DIVINE GUIDANCE

    Being led by the spirit of God is one of the most important aspects of a believer's life. I cannot tell you how many times my life has been spared because I heard the voice of God. Jesus is very emphatic when he declares that my sheep hear my voice, and another they will not follow. It is extremely important that we become very sensitive to what God is saying to us 1st of all through his word. I actually have written a book about the 20 ways in which God leads and guides his people. Of course one of the major ways that God speaks to us is through his word. As you hide the Scriptures in your heart, meditating upon them, they will become alive on the inside of you . The Holy Spirit will use them to lead and guide you in the exact direction that you need to hear from the heavenly father.

*Psalms 32:8 - I will instruct thee and teach thee in the way which thou shalt go: I will guide thee with mine eye.

---

*John 16:13 - Howbeit when he, the Spirit of truth, is come, he will guide you into all truth: for he shall not speak of himself; but whatsoever he shall hear, [that] shall he speak: and he will shew you things to come.

---

*Proverbs 3:5-6 - Trust in the LORD with all thine heart; and lean not unto thine own understanding. 6 In all thy ways acknowledge him, and he shall direct thy paths.

---

*Psalms 119:105 Thy word [is] a lamp unto my feet, and a light unto my path.

---

*Psalm 18:28 For thou wilt light my candle: the Lord my God will enlighten my darkness.

*Amos 3:7 Surely the Lord God will do nothing, but he revealeth his secret unto his servants the prophets.

*John 15:15 Henceforth I call you not servants; for the servant knoweth not what his lord doeth: but I have called you friends; for all things that I have heard of my Father I have made known unto you.

*Psalm 25:14 The secret of the Lord is with them that fear him; and he will shew them his covenant.

*Jeremiah 23:22 But if they had stood in my counsel, and had caused my people to hear my words, then they should have turned them from their evil way, and from the evil of their doings.

*1 Corinthians 14:24 But if all prophesy, and there come in one that believeth not, or one unlearned, he is convinced of all, he is judged of all: 25 and thus are the secrets of his heart made manifest; and so falling down on his face he will worship God, and report that God is in you of a truth.

*John 14:26 - But the Comforter, [which is] the Holy Ghost, whom the Father will send in my name, he shall teach you all things, and bring all things to your remembrance, whatsoever I have said unto you.

---

*James 1:5-6 - If any of you lack wisdom, let him ask of God, that giveth to all [men] liberally, and upbraideth not; and it shall be given him.

---

*Psalms 37:23-24 - The steps of a [good] man are ordered by the LORD: and he delighteth in his way.

---

*Psalms 25:9-10 - The meek will he guide in judgment: and the meek will he teach his way.

---

*2 Timothy 3:16 - All scripture [is] given by inspiration of God, and [is] profitable for doctrine, for reproof, for correction, for instruction in righteousness:

---

*Isaiah 30:21 - And thine ears shall hear a word behind thee, saying, This [is] the way, walk ye in it, when ye turn to the right hand, and when ye turn to the left.

---

*Psalms 25:4-5 - Shew me thy ways, O LORD; teach me thy paths.

---

*1 Peter 4:11 - If any man speak, [let him speak] as the oracles of God; if any man minister, [let him do it] as of the ability which God giveth: that God in all things may be glorified through Jesus Christ, to whom be praise and dominion for ever and ever. Amen.

---

*Psalms 37:23 - The steps of a [good] man are ordered by the LORD: and he delighteth in his way.

---

*Psalms 25:5-9 - Lead me in thy truth, and teach me: for thou [art] the God of my salvation; on thee do I wait all the day.

---

*1 Corinthians 1:30 - But of him are ye in Christ Jesus, who of God is made unto us wisdom, and righteousness, and sanctification, and redemption:

---

*Psalms 25:12-15 - What man [is] he that feareth the LORD? him shall he teach in the way [that] he shall choose.

---

*Job 33:14-15 - For God speaketh once, yea twice, [yet man] perceiveth it not.

---

*Isaiah 11:2 - And the spirit of the LORD shall rest upon him, the spirit of wisdom and understanding, the spirit of counsel and might, the spirit of knowledge and of the fear of the LORD;

*Psalm 73:24 Thou shalt guide me with thy counsel, and afterward receive me to glory.

*Isaiah 58:11 and the Lord shall guide thee continually, and satisfy thy soul in drought, and make fat thy bones: and thou shalt be like a watered garden, and like a spring of water, whose waters fail not.

*Luke 1:78 through the tender mercy of our God;whereby the dayspring from on high hath visited us,79 to give light to them that sit in darkness and in the shadow of death,to guide our feet into the way of peace.

*Proverbs 6:21 bind them continually upon thine heart,and tie them about thy neck.22 When thou goest, it shall lead thee;when thou sleepest, it shall keep thee;and when thou awakest, it shall talk with thee.23 For the commandment is a lamp; and the law is light;and reproofs of instruction are the way of life:

*Isaiah 42:16 And I will bring the blind by a way that they knew not; I will lead them in paths that they have not known: I will make darkness light before them, and crooked things straight. These things will I do unto them, and not forsake them.

*Matthew 6:13 And lead us not into temptation, but deliver us from evil: For thine is the kingdom, and the power, and the glory, for ever. Amen.

---

*Revelation 7:17 For the Lamb which is in the midst of the throne shall feed them, and shall lead them unto living fountains of waters: and God shall wipe away all tears from their eyes.

---

*Proverbs 3:5 Trust in the Lord with all thine heart; and lean not unto thine own understanding.6 In all thy ways acknowledge him, and he shall direct thy paths.

---

*Jeremiah 10:23 O Lord, I know that the way of man is not in himself: it is not in man that walketh to direct his steps.

---

*2 Peter 1:21 For the prophecy came not in old time by the will of man: but holy men of God spake as they were moved by the Holy Ghost.

---

*Romans 8:14 For as many as are led by the Spirit of God, they are the sons of God.

---

*Romans 8:5 For they that are after the flesh do mind the things of the flesh; but they that are after the Spirit the things of the Spirit.

*Psalm 143:10 Teach me to do thy will; for thou art my God: thy spirit is good; lead me into the land of uprightness.

*Proverbs 8:20 I lead in the way of righteousness, in the midst of the paths of judgment:

*Proverbs 20:27 The spirit of man is the candle of the Lord, searching all the inward parts of the belly.

*Psalm 16:11 Thou wilt shew me the path of life: in thy presence is fulness of joy; at thy right hand there are pleasures for evermore.

Courage

*Deuteronomy 31:6 - Be strong and of a good courage, fear not, nor be afraid of them: for the LORD thy God, he [it is] that doth go with thee; he will not fail thee, nor forsake thee.

*Psalm 27:1 The Lord is my light and my salvation; whom shall I fear? the Lord is the strength of my life; of whom shall I be afraid?

*2 Timothy 1:7 - For God hath not given us the spirit of fear; but of power, and of love, and of a sound mind.

*Psalm 56:4 In God I will praise his word, in God I have put my trust; I will not fear what flesh can do unto me.

*1 Corinthians 16:13 - Watch ye, stand fast in the faith, quit you like men, be strong.

*Jeremiah 1:8 Be not afraid of their faces: for I am with thee to deliver thee, saith the Lord.

*John 16:33 - These things I have spoken unto you, that in me ye might have peace. In the world ye shall have tribulation: but be of good cheer; I have overcome the world.

*Psalm 118:6 The Lord is on my side; I will not fear: what can man do unto me?

*Proverbs 28:1 - The wicked flee when no man pursueth: but the righteous are bold as a lion.

*Isaiah 41:10 Fear thou not; for I am with thee: be not dismayed; for I am thy God: I will strengthen thee; yea, I will help thee; yea, I will uphold thee with the right hand of my righteousness.

*Joshua 1:9 - Have not I commanded thee? Be strong and of a good courage; be not afraid, neither be thou dismayed: for the LORD thy God [is] with thee whithersoever thou goest.

*Isaiah 54:4 Fear not; for thou shalt not be ashamed: neither be thou confounded; for thou shalt not be put to shame: for thou shalt forget the shame of thy youth, and shalt not remember the reproach of thy widowhood any more.

*1 Chronicles 28:20 - And David said to Solomon his son, Be strong and of good courage, and do [it]: fear not, nor be dismayed: for the LORD God, [even] my God, [will be] with thee; he will not fail thee, nor forsake thee, until thou hast finished all the work for the service of the house of the LORD.

*Philippians 1:28 - And in nothing terrified by your adversaries: which is to them an evident token of perdition, but to you of salvation, and that of God.

*1 Corinthians 10:13 - There hath no temptation taken you but such as is common to man: but God [is] faithful, who will not suffer you to be tempted above that ye are able; but will with the temptation also make a way to escape, that ye may be able to bear [it].

*Psalms 27:14 - Wait on the LORD: be of good courage, and he shall strengthen thine heart: wait, I say, on the LORD.

---

*Psalms 31:24 - Be of good courage, and he shall strengthen your heart, all ye that hope in the LORD.

---

*Ephesians 6:10-18 - Finally, my brethren, be strong in the Lord, and in the power of his might.   (Read More...)

---

*Matthew 10:16-20 - Behold, I send you forth as sheep in the midst of wolves: be ye therefore wise as serpents, and harmless as doves.

---

*Romans 8:31-39 ...If God [be] for us, who [can be] against us?

---

*Acts 5:29 - Then Peter and the [other] apostles answered and said, We ought to obey God rather than men.

---

*John 10:27 My sheep hear my voice, and I know them, and they follow me:

CHAPTER SEVEN
AUTHORITY & POWER

Those who know Christ are called of God to walk in a place of authority and power. These I share with you are powerful Scriptures that we need to meditate upon on a daily basis in order to step into this reality. I have included a combination of old and new Testaments Scriptures that will help you to begin to realize this amazing place where Christ has call us to walk and move.

*Daniel 11:32 ..... but the people that do know their God shall be strong, and do exploits.

*Jeremiah 33:3 call unto me, and I will answer thee, and shew thee great and mighty things, which thou knowest not.

*Isaiah 65:24 And it shall come to pass, that before they call, I will answer; and while they are yet speaking, I will hear.

*Ephesians 3:20 Now unto him that is able to do exceeding abundantly above all that we ask or think, according to the power that worketh in us,

*Isaiah 55:6 Seek ye the Lord while he may be found, call ye upon him while he is near:7 Let the wicked forsake his way, and the unrighteous man his thoughts: and let him return unto the Lord, and he will have mercy upon him; and to our God, for he will abundantly pardon.

*Isaiah 45:3 And I will give thee the treasures of darkness, and hidden riches of secret places, that thou mayest know that I, the Lord, which call thee by thy name, am the God of Israel.

---

*Psalm 25:14 The secret of the Lord is with them that fear him; and he will shew them his covenant.

---

*1 Peter 4:11 If any man speak, let him speak as the oracles of God; if any man minister, let him do it as of the ability which God giveth: that God in all things may be glorified through Jesus Christ, to whom be praise and dominion for ever and ever. Amen.

---

*Acts 1:8 But ye shall receive power, after that the Holy Ghost is come upon you: and ye shall be witnesses unto me both in Jerusalem, and in all Judæa, and in Samaria, and unto the uttermost part of the earth.

---

*Proverbs 28:1 The wicked flee when no man pursueth: but the righteous are bold as a lion.

---

*2 Samuel 23:2 The Spirit of the Lord spake by me, and his word was in my tongue.

---

*Acts 10:38 how God anointed Jesus of Nazareth with the Holy Ghost and with power: who went about doing good, and healing all that were oppressed of the devil; for God was with him.

---

*Matthew 10:8 Heal the sick, cleanse the lepers, raise the dead, cast out devils: freely ye have received, freely give.

---

*Luke 4:18 The Spirit of the Lord is upon me, because he hath anointed me to preach the gospel to the poor; he hath sent me to heal the brokenhearted, to preach deliverance to the captives, and recovering of sight to the blind, to set at liberty them that are bruised, 19 to preach the acceptable year of the Lord.

---

*Numbers 23:19 God is not a man, that he should lie; neither the son of man, that he should repent: hath he said, and shall he not do it? or hath he spoken, and shall he not make it good?

---

*Acts 6:8 And Stephen, full of faith and power, did great wonders and miracles among the people.

---

*Acts 2:17 And it shall come to pass in the last days, saith God, I will pour out of my Spirit upon all flesh: and your sons and your daughters shall prophesy, and your young men shall see visions, and your old men shall dream dreams:18 And on my servants and on my handmaidens I will pour out in those days of my Spirit; and they shall prophesy:

*Luke 10:19 Behold, I give unto you power to tread on serpents and scorpions, and over all the power of the enemy: and nothing shall by any means hurt you.

*2 Samuel 22:35 He teacheth my hands to war; so that a bow of steel is broken by mine arms.

*Psalm 18:33 He maketh my feet like hinds' feet, and setteth me upon my high places.34 He teacheth my hands to war, so that a bow of steel is broken by mine arms.

*Matthew 8:9 For I am a man under authority, having soldiers under me: and I say to this man, Go, and he goeth; and to another, Come, and he cometh; and to my servant, Do this, and he doeth it.

*Mark 1:27 And they were all amazed, insomuch that they questioned among themselves, saying, What thing is this? what new doctrine is this? for with authority commandeth he even the unclean spirits, and they do obey him.

*Luke 9:1 Then he called his twelve disciples together, and gave them power and authority over all devils, and to cure diseases.

Protection

*Psalm 34:19 Many are the afflictions of the righteous: but the Lord delivereth him out of them all.

*Isaiah 54:17 - No weapon that is formed against thee shall prosper; and every tongue [that] shall rise against thee in judgment thou shalt condemn. This [is] the heritage of the servants of the LORD, and their righteousness [is] of me, saith the LORD.

*2 Samuel 22:3 the God of my rock; in him will I trust: he is my shield, and the horn of my salvation, my high tower, and my refuge, my saviour; thou savest me from violence.

*Psalms 91:1 He that dwelleth in the secret place of the most High shall abide under the shadow of the Almighty.

*Psalm 4:8 I will both lay me down in peace, and sleep: for thou, Lord, only makest me dwell in safety.

*Jude 1:24-25 - Now unto him that is able to keep you from falling, and to present [you] faultless before the presence of his glory with exceeding joy,

*Psalm 62:2 He only is my rock and my salvation; he is my defence; I shall not be greatly moved.

*Isaiah 26:3-4 - Thou wilt keep [him] in perfect peace, [whose] mind [is] stayed [on thee]: because he trusteth in thee.

*Psalm 91:4 He shall cover thee with his feathers, and under his wings shalt thou trust: his truth shall be thy shield and buckler.

*1 Peter 2:9 - But ye [are] a chosen generation, a royal priesthood, an holy nation, a peculiar people; that ye should shew forth the praises of him who hath called you out of darkness into his marvellous light:

*John 10:10 - The thief cometh not, but for to steal, and to kill, and to destroy: I am come that they might have life, and that they might have [it] more abundantly.

*John 8:32 - And ye shall know the truth, and the truth shall make you free.

*Psalms 121:1 I will lift up mine eyes unto the hills, from whence cometh my help.

*Psalms 46:1 God [is] our refuge and strength, a very present help in trouble.

*Hebrews 4:16 - Let us therefore come boldly unto the throne of grace, that we may obtain mercy, and find grace to help in time of need.

*1 John 3:8 ..... For this purpose the Son of God was manifested, that he might destroy the works of the devil.

*Philippians 4:19 - But my God shall supply all your need according to his riches in glory by Christ Jesus.

*Ephesians 1:3 - Blessed [be] the God and Father of our Lord Jesus Christ, who hath blessed us with all spiritual blessings in heavenly [places] in Christ:

*Isaiah 43:2 When thou passest through the waters, I will be with thee; and through the rivers, they shall not overflow thee: when thou walkest through the fire, thou shalt not be burned; neither shall the flame kindle upon thee.

CHAPTER EIGHT
FAITH, TRUST, BELIEVE,

Faith in **Christ** is the key to our victory! With this truth and reality in our heart, it is expedient that we become full of faith. As we connect the dots from Genesis to Revelation, it becomes quite clear that the cause of all of man's sorrows, shortcomings, immoralities, sicknesses, troubles are due to the fact that we are not truly trusting, looking, depending, relying and having faith in **Christ**! Based upon this fact we must do everything we can to attain more faith. Even the disciples as they watched the life of **Jesus** before their eyes, asked Him to help increase their faith. This is the whole purpose of this book. To provide biblical means by which we can have an increase of faith in **Christ** which causes us to overcome! Please open your heart, your mind, and your life to these realities. And let **Jesus Christ** become your all!

A Brief Description of Faith: It is when God, His Word, His will is Supernaturally Quickened to you by the Holy Spirit! These realities become more real to you than anything in life. It is a revelation of Who Jesus Christ really is & what He has done and is doing. It is a quickening in your heart when you know, that you know, that you know, that you know God is with you, then who can be against you? That Christ Jesus Himself, lives inside of you. Your mind, your will, your emotions, and every part of your being is overwhelmed with the reality of Jesus Christ! And you enter into the realm where all things are possible! This is where, by God's grace it is my hope and desire to take you.

*Proverbs 3:Trust in the Lord with all thine heart; and lean not unto thine own understanding. In all thy ways acknowledge him, and he shall direct thy paths.

---

*2 Corinthians 5:7 - (For we walk by faith, not by sight:)

---

*Hebrews 11:6 - But without faith [it is] impossible to please [him]: for he that cometh to God must believe that he is, and [that] he is a rewarder of them that diligently seek him.

*1 John 5:4 - For whatsoever is born of God overcometh the world: and this is the victory that overcometh the world, [even] our faith.

*Mark 9:23 - Jesus said unto him, If thou canst believe, all things [are] possible to him that believeth.

*Luke 17:6 - And the Lord said, If ye had faith as a grain of mustard seed, ye might say unto this sycamine tree, Be thou plucked up by the root, and be thou planted in the sea; and it should obey you.

*Hebrews 11:1-39 - Now faith is the substance of things hoped for, the evidence of things not seen.

*1 John 5:14 - And this is the confidence that we have in him, that, if we ask any thing according to his will, he heareth us:

*Philippians 4:13 - I can do all things through Christ which strengtheneth me.

*Hebrews 11:1 - Now faith is the substance of things hoped for, the evidence of things not seen.

*Psalms 40:4 - Blessed [is] that man that maketh the LORD his trust, and respecteth not the proud, nor such as turn aside to lies.

*Mark 11:23 - For verily I say unto you, That whosoever shall say unto this mountain, Be thou removed, and be thou cast into the sea; and shall not doubt in his heart, but shall believe that those things which he saith shall come to pass; he shall have whatsoever he saith.

*John 3:36 - He that believeth on the Son hath everlasting life: and he that believeth not the Son shall not see life; but the wrath of God abideth on him.

*Acts 26:18 - To open their eyes, [and] to turn [them] from darkness to light, and [from] the power of Satan unto God, that they may receive forgiveness of sins, and inheritance among them which are sanctified by faith that is in me.

*James 1:12 - Blessed [is] the man that endureth temptation: for when he is tried, he shall receive the crown of life, which the Lord hath promised to them that love him.

*1 Peter 1:7 - That the trial of your faith, being much more precious than of gold that perisheth, though it be tried with fire, might be found unto praise and honour and glory at the appearing of Jesus Christ:

*Ephesians 6:16 - Above all, taking the shield of faith, wherewith ye shall be able to quench all the fiery darts of the wicked.

*1 Corinthians 2:5 - That your faith should not stand in the wisdom of men, but in the power of God.

*Isaiah 40:31 - But they that wait upon the LORD shall renew [their] strength; they shall mount up with wings as eagles; they shall run, and not be weary; [and] they shall walk, and not faint.

*Ephesians 6:10-18 - Finally, my brethren, be strong in the Lord, and in the power of his might.   (Read More...)

*Colossians 2:7 - Rooted and built up in him, and stablished in the faith, as ye have been taught, abounding therein with thanksgiving.

*1 Samuel 17:37 - David said moreover, The LORD that delivered me out of the paw of the lion, and out of the paw of the bear, he will deliver me out of the hand of this Philistine. And Saul said unto David, Go, and the LORD be with thee.

*Revelation 3:20 - Behold, I stand at the door, and knock: if any man hear my voice, and open the door, I will come in to him, and will sup with him, and he with me.

*Hebrews 10:39 - But we are not of them who draw back unto perdition; but of them that believe to the saving of the soul.

*Romans 8:37 - Nay, in all these things we are more than conquerors through him that loved us.

*James 1:6 - But let him ask in faith, nothing wavering. For he that wavereth is like a wave of the sea driven with the wind and tossed.

*Hebrews 11:7 - By faith Noah, being warned of God of things not seen as yet, moved with fear, prepared an ark to the saving of his house; by the which he condemned the world, and became heir of the righteousness which is by faith.

*2 Timothy 4:7 - I have fought a good fight, I have finished [my] course, I have kept the faith:

*Mark 16:16 - He that believeth and is baptized shall be saved; but he that believeth not shall be damned.

*Hebrews 12:2 - Looking unto Jesus the author and finisher of [our] faith; who for the joy that was set before him endured the cross, despising the shame, and is set down at the right hand of the throne of God.

*1 Timothy 3:9 - Holding the mystery of the faith in a pure conscience.

*Colossians 1:23 - If ye continue in the faith grounded and settled, and [be] not moved away from the hope of the gospel, which ye have heard, [and] which was preached to every creature which is under heaven; whereof I Paul am made a minister;

*Romans 10:17 - So then faith [cometh] by hearing, and hearing by the word of God.

*1 Peter 1:8 - Whom having not seen, ye love; in whom, though now ye see [him] not, yet believing, ye rejoice with joy unspeakable and full of glory:

*John 6:35 - And Jesus said unto them, I am the bread of life: he that cometh to me shall never hunger; and he that believeth on me shall never thirst.

*Colossians 2:7 - Rooted and built up in him, and stablished in the faith, as ye have been taught, abounding therein with thanksgiving.

*Romans 10:9 - That if thou shalt confess with thy mouth the Lord Jesus, and shalt believe in thine heart that God hath raised him from the dead, thou shalt be saved.

*Psalms 40:4 - Blessed [is] that man that maketh the LORD his trust, and respecteth not the proud, nor such as turn aside to lies.

*Psalms 60:12 - Through God we shall do valiantly: for he [it is that] shall tread down our enemies.

*Psalms 31:14-15 - But I trusted in thee, O LORD: I said, Thou [art] my God.

*Galatians 5:1 - Stand fast therefore in the liberty wherewith Christ hath made us free, and be not entangled again with the yoke of bondage.

*Isaiah 40:31 - But they that wait upon the LORD shall renew [their] strength; they shall mount up with wings as eagles; they shall run, and not be weary; [and] they shall walk, and not faint.

*Isaiah 26:3-4 - Thou wilt keep [him] in perfect peace, [whose] mind [is] stayed [on thee]: because he trusteth in thee.

*Psalms 37:5-6 - Commit thy way unto the LORD; trust also in him; and he shall bring [it] to pass.

*Mark 11:24 - Therefore I say unto you, What things soever ye desire, when ye pray, believe that ye receive [them], and ye shall have [them].

*Psalm 57:1 Be merciful unto me, O God, be merciful unto me: for my soul trusteth in thee: yea, in the shadow of thy wings will I make my refuge, until these calamities be overpast.

*1 Timothy 6:12 Fight the good fight of faith, lay hold on eternal life, whereunto thou art also called, and hast professed a good profession before many witnesses.

*2 Timothy 4:7 I have fought a good fight, I have finished my course, I have kept the faith:

Purpose & Calling

*Matthew 4:19 And he saith unto them, Follow me, and I will make you fishers of men.

*Jeremiah 1:5 Before I formed thee in the belly I knew thee; and before thou camest forth out of the womb I sanctified thee, and I ordained thee a prophet unto the nations.

*Philippians 3:14 I press toward the mark for the prize of the high calling of God in Christ Jesus.

*1 Peter 5:2 feed the flock of God which is among you, taking the oversight thereof, not by constraint, but willingly; not for filthy lucre, but of a ready mind;

*2 Timothy 4:2 preach the word; be instant in season, out of season; reprove, rebuke, exhort with all longsuffering and doctrine.

*1 Corinthians 7:20 Let every man abide in the same calling wherein he was called.

*John 15:16 Ye have not chosen me, but I have chosen you, and ordained you, that ye should go and bring forth fruit, and that your fruit should remain: that whatsoever ye shall ask of the Father in my name, he may give it you.

---

*1 Peter 4:11 If any man speak, let him speak as the oracles of God; if any man minister, let him do it as of the ability which God giveth: that God in all things may be glorified through Jesus Christ, to whom be praise and dominion for ever and ever. Amen.

---

*Ephesians 1:4 - According as he hath chosen us in him before the foundation of the world, that we should be holy and without blame before him in love:

---

*Colossians 2:9 - For in him dwelleth all the fulness of the Godhead bodily.

---

*Ephesians 4:1-15 - I therefore, the prisoner of the Lord, beseech you that ye walk worthy of the vocation wherewith ye are called,

---

*1 Corinthians 6:19-20 - What? know ye not that your body is the temple of the Holy Ghost [which is] in you, which ye have of God, and ye are not your own?

---

*Matthew 6:19-21 - Lay not up for yourselves treasures upon earth, where moth and rust doth corrupt, and where thieves break through and steal:

---

*Galatians 2:20 - I am crucified with Christ: nevertheless I live; yet not I, but Christ liveth in me: and the life which I now live in the flesh I live by the faith of the Son of God, who loved me, and gave himself for me.

---

*Luke 16:13 - No servant can serve two masters: for either he will hate the one, and love the other; or else he will hold to the one, and despise the other. Ye cannot serve God and mammon.

---

*Mark 16:16 - He that believeth and is baptized shall be saved; but he that believeth not shall be damned.

---

*Genesis 1:27 - So God created man in his [own] image, in the image of God created he him; male and female created he them.

---

*Romans 12:4 - For as we have many members in one body, and all members have not the same office:

---

*Jeremiah 29:11 - For I know the thoughts that I think toward you, saith the LORD, thoughts of peace, and not of evil, to give you an expected end.

*John 14:6 - Jesus saith unto him, I am the way, the truth, and the life: no man cometh unto the Father, but by me.

*1 Peter 2:9 - But ye [are] a chosen generation, a royal priesthood, an holy nation, a peculiar people; that ye should shew forth the praises of him who hath called you out of darkness into his marvellous light:

*Colossians 1:16 - For by him were all things created, that are in heaven, and that are in earth, visible and invisible, whether [they be] thrones, or dominions, or principalities, or powers: all things were created by him, and for him:

*Matthew 28:18-20 - And Jesus came and spake unto them, saying, All power is given unto me in heaven and in earth.

*Isaiah 46:10 - Declaring the end from the beginning, and from ancient times [the things] that are not [yet] done, saying, My counsel shall stand, and I will do all my pleasure:

*Revelation 4:11 - Thou art worthy, O Lord, to receive glory and honour and power: for thou hast created all things, and for thy pleasure they are and were created.

CHAPTER NINE
MANY PROMISES

According to one biblical source, there are over **3500** promises in the Bible. God has provided many prophetic promises to his people in order to meet every one of their needs. Of course this little book is only a small fraction of these promises that God has given to us. All the promises in Christ are yea and amen to the believer who would choose to believe what God says is true. This is one reason why we can cast all of our cares upon him, because he cares for us.

Blessings

*James 1:17 - Every good gift and every perfect gift is from above, and cometh down from the Father of lights, with whom is no variableness, neither shadow of turning.

---

*Luke 6:38 - Give, and it shall be given unto you; good measure, pressed down, and shaken together, and running over, shall men give into your bosom. For with the same measure that ye mete withal it shall be measured to you again.

---

*3 John 1:2 - Beloved, I wish above all things that thou mayest prosper and be in health, even as thy soul prospereth.

---

*Isaiah 41:10 - Fear thou not; for I [am] with thee: be not dismayed; for I [am] thy God: I will strengthen thee; yea, I will help thee; yea, I will uphold thee with the right hand of my righteousness.

---

*John 1:16 - And of his fulness have all we received, and grace for grace.

*Philippians 2:13 - For it is God which worketh in you both to will and to do of [his] good pleasure.

*2 Chronicles 27:6 - So Jotham became mighty, because he prepared his ways before the LORD his God.

*Philippians 4:7 - And the peace of God, which passeth all understanding, shall keep your hearts and minds through Christ Jesus.

*Philippians 1:6 - Being confident of this very thing, that he which hath begun a good work in you will perform [it] until the day of Jesus Christ:

*2 Corinthians 9:8 And God [is] able to make all grace abound toward you; that ye, always having all sufficiency in all [things], may abound to every good work:

*1 Corinthians 15:10 - But by the grace of God I am what I am: and his grace which [was bestowed] upon me was not in vain; but I laboured more abundantly than they all: yet not I, but the grace of God which was with me.

*Matthew 24:13 - But he that shall endure unto the end, the same shall be saved.

*Hebrews 10:36 - For ye have need of patience, that, after ye have done the will of God, ye might receive the promise.

Malachi 3:2 - But who may abide the day of his coming? and who shall stand when he appeareth? for he [is] like a refiner's fire, and like fullers' soap:

*Habakkuk 3:19 - The LORD God [is] my strength, and he will make my feet like hinds' [feet], and he will make me to walk upon mine high places.

*Isaiah 40:31 - But they that wait upon the LORD shall renew [their] strength; they shall mount up with wings as eagles; they shall run, and not be weary; [and] they shall walk, and not faint.

*1 John 4:4 - Ye are of God, little children, and have overcome them: because greater is he that is in you, than he that is in the world.

*Ephesians 1:3 - Blessed [be] the God and Father of our Lord Jesus Christ, who hath blessed us with all spiritual blessings in heavenly [places] in Christ:

---

*Isaiah 1:19 - If ye be willing and obedient, ye shall eat the good of the land:

---

*Psalms 127:5-9 - Happy [is] the man that hath his quiver full of them: they shall not be ashamed…

---

*Deuteronomy 28:1And it shall come to pass, if thou shalt hearken diligently unto the voice of the LORD thy God, to observe [and] to do all his commandments which I command thee this day, that the LORD thy God will set thee on high above all nations of the earth:

---

*Psalm 84:11 For the Lord God is a sun and shield: the Lord will give grace and glory: no good thing will he withhold from them that walk uprightly.

---

*James 1:18 - Of his own will begat he us with the word of truth, that we should be a kind of firstfruits of his creatures.

---

*2 Corinthians 10:4 - (For the weapons of our warfare [are] not carnal, but mighty through God to the pulling down of strong holds;)

---

*Zechariah 10:1 - Ask ye of the LORD rain in the time of the latter rain; [so] the LORD shall make bright clouds, and give them showers of rain, to every one grass in the field.

Provision

*Deuteronomy 8:18 But thou shalt remember the Lord thy God: for it is he that giveth thee power to get wealth, that he may establish his covenant which he sware unto thy fathers, as it is this day.

---

*Proverbs 3:5 - Trust in the LORD with all thine heart; and lean not unto thine own understanding.

---

*Hebrews 13:5 - [Let your] conversation [be] without covetousness; [and be] content with such things as ye have: for he hath said, I will never leave thee, nor forsake thee.

---

*2 Peter 1:3 - According as his divine power hath given unto us all things that [pertain] unto life and godliness, through the knowledge of him that hath called us to glory and virtue:

---

*Philippians 1:6 - Being confident of this very thing, that he which hath begun a good work in you will perform [it] until the day of Jesus Christ:

---

*Matthew 11:28 - Come unto me, all [ye] that labour and are heavy laden, and I will give you rest.

---

*Philippians 2:12-13 - Wherefore, my beloved, as ye have always obeyed, not as in my presence only, but now much more in my absence, work out your own salvation with fear and trembling.

---

*2 Corinthians 5:21 - For he hath made him [to be] sin for us, who knew no sin; that we might be made the righteousness of God in him.

---

*Romans 3:23-26 - For all have sinned, and come short of the glory of God;

---

*2 Corinthians 1:20 For all the promises of God in him are yea, and in him Amen, unto the glory of God by us.

Overcomes

*Romans 12:21 Be not overcome of evil, but overcome evil with good.

*Revelation 3:21 - To him that overcometh will I grant to sit with me in my throne, even as I also overcame, and am set down with my Father in his throne.

*1 John 5:1-21 - Whosoever believeth that Jesus is the Christ is born of God: and every one that loveth him that begat loveth him also that is begotten of him.

*Matthew 7:21-23 - Not every one that saith unto me, Lord, Lord, shall enter into the kingdom of heaven; but he that doeth the will of my Father which is in heaven.

*1 John 5:3 - For this is the love of God, that we keep his commandments: and his commandments are not grievous.

*Hebrews 4:16 - Let us therefore come boldly unto the throne of grace, that we may obtain mercy, and find grace to help in time of need.

*John 12:31 - Now is the judgment of this world: now shall the prince of this world be cast out.

*Jeremiah 17:9 - The heart [is] deceitful above all [things], and desperately wicked: who can know it?

---

*Isaiah 55:7 - Let the wicked forsake his way, and the unrighteous man his thoughts: and let him return unto the LORD, and he will have mercy upon him; and to our God, for he will abundantly pardon.

---

*Revelation 2:26 - And he that overcometh, and keepeth my works unto the end, to him will I give power over the nations:

CHAPTER TEN
IMPORTANT SCRIPTURES

<u>*Forgiveness*</u>

*Ephesians 4:32 - And be ye kind one to another, tenderhearted, forgiving one another, even as God for Christ's sake hath forgiven you.

---

*Mark 11:25 - And when ye stand praying, forgive, if ye have ought against any: that your Father also which is in heaven may forgive you your trespasses.

---

*1 John 1:9 - If we confess our sins, he is faithful and just to forgive us [our] sins, and to cleanse us from all unrighteousness.

---

*Matthew 6:14-15 - For if ye forgive men their trespasses, your heavenly Father will also forgive you:

---

*Matthew 7:21-23 - Not every one that saith unto me, Lord, Lord, shall enter into the kingdom of heaven; but he that doeth the will of my Father which is in heaven.

---

*2 Corinthians 7:1 - Having therefore these promises, dearly beloved, let us cleanse ourselves from all filthiness of the flesh and spirit, perfecting holiness in the fear of God.

Praise, Worship, Thanksgiving,

*Philippians 4:6 - Be careful for nothing; but in every thing by prayer and supplication with thanksgiving let your requests be made known unto God.

---

*Psalms 7:17 - I will praise the LORD according to his righteousness: and will sing praise to the name of the LORD most high.

---

*1 Thessalonians 5:18 - In every thing give thanks: for this is the will of God in Christ Jesus concerning you.

---

*Psalms 107:1 - O give thanks unto the LORD, for [he is] good: for his mercy [endureth] for ever.

---

*Ephesians 5:20 - Giving thanks always for all things unto God and the Father in the name of our Lord Jesus Christ;

---

*Psalms 50:14 - Offer unto God thanksgiving; and pay thy vows unto the most High:

---

*Psalms 100:1 Make a joyful noise unto the LORD, all ye lands.

*Hebrews 13:15 - By him therefore let us offer the sacrifice of praise to God continually, that is, the fruit of [our] lips giving thanks to his name.

---

*Luke 6:38 - Give, and it shall be given unto you; good measure, pressed down, and shaken together, and running over, shall men give into your bosom. For with the same measure that ye *Colossians 3:15 - And let the peace of God rule in your hearts, to the which also ye are called in one body; and be ye thankful.

---

*Habakkuk 3:17 - Although the fig tree shall not blossom, neither [shall] fruit [be] in the vines; the labour of the olive shall fail, and the fields shall yield no meat; the flock shall be cut off from the fold, and [there shall be] no herd in the stalls:

---

*Psalms 92:1[It is a] good [thing] to give thanks unto the LORD, and to sing praises unto thy name, O most High:

---

*1 Thessalonians 5:17 - Pray without ceasing.

---

*Psalms 95:6 - O come, let us worship and bow down: let us kneel before the LORD our maker.

---

*Matthew 18:20 - For where two or three are gathered together in my name, there am I in the midst of them.

*John 4:23 - But the hour cometh, and now is, when the true worshippers shall worship the Father in spirit and in truth: for the Father seeketh such to worship him.

*Psalms 29:2 - Give unto the LORD the glory due unto his name; worship the LORD in the beauty of holiness.

*1 Peter 2:5 - Ye also, as lively stones, are built up a spiritual house, an holy priesthood, to offer up spiritual sacrifices, acceptable to God by Jesus Christ.

*Psalms 96:9 - O worship the LORD in the beauty of holiness: fear before him, all the earth.

*Psalms 95:1-6 - O come, let us sing unto the LORD: let us make a joyful noise to the rock of our salvation.

*Psalms 96:8 - Give unto the LORD the glory [due unto] his name: bring an offering, and come into his courts.

*Acts 16:25 – And at midnight Paul and Silas prayed, and sang praises unto God: and the prisoners heard them.

The Fear of the Lord

*Philippians 2:12 Wherefore, my beloved, as ye have always obeyed, not as in my presence only, but now much more in my absence, work out your own salvation with fear and trembling.

*Proverbs 8:13 - The fear of the LORD [is] to hate evil: pride, and arrogancy, and the evil way, and the froward mouth, do I hate.

*Proverbs 1:7 - The fear of the LORD [is] the beginning of knowledge:

*Matthew 10:28 - And fear not them which kill the body, but are not able to kill the soul: but rather fear him which is able to destroy both soul and body in hell.

*Psalms 33:8 - Let all the earth fear the LORD: let all the inhabitants of the world stand in awe of him.

*Proverbs 14:27 - The fear of the LORD [is] a fountain of life, to depart from the snares of death.

*Psalms 25:14 - The secret of the LORD [is] with them that fear him; and he will shew them his covenant.

*Deuteronomy 10:12 - And now, Israel, what doth the LORD thy God require of thee, but to fear the LORD thy God, to walk in all his ways, and to love him, and to serve the LORD thy God with all thy heart and with all thy soul,

*Proverbs 16:6 - By mercy and truth iniquity is purged: and by the fear of the LORD [men] depart from evil.

*Psalms 19:9 - The fear of the LORD [is] clean, enduring for ever: the judgments of the LORD [are] true [and] righteous altogether.

*1 Peter 1:17 - And if ye call on the Father, who without respect of persons judgeth according to every man's work, pass the time of your sojourning [here] in fear:

*Ephesians 5:21 - Submitting yourselves one to another in the fear of God.

*Proverbs 14:16 - A wise [man] feareth, and departeth from evil: but the fool rageth, and is confident.

*2 Timothy 1:7 - For God hath not given us the spirit of fear; but of power, and of love, and of a sound mind.

Our Enemy the devil

*1 Peter 5:8 - Be sober, be vigilant; because your adversary the devil, as a roaring lion, walketh about, seeking whom he may devour:

---

*Hebrews 2:14 - Forasmuch then as the children are partakers of flesh and blood, he also himself likewise took part of the same; that through death he might destroy him that had the power of death, that is, the devil;

---

*2 Corinthians 11:14 - And no marvel; for Satan himself is transformed into an angel of light.

---

*2 Corinthians 10:3-5 - For though we walk in the flesh, we do not war after the flesh:

---

*Ephesians 6:12 For we wrestle not against flesh and blood, but against principalities, against powers, against the rulers of the darkness of this world, against spiritual wickedness in high places. 13 Wherefore take unto you the whole armour of God, that ye may be able to withstand in the evil day, and having done all, to stand.

---

*John 10:10 - The thief cometh not, but for to steal, and to kill, and to destroy: I am come that they might have life, and that they might have [it] more abundantly.

---

*John 8:44 - Ye are of [your] father the devil, and the lusts of your father ye will do. He was a murderer from the beginning, and abode not in the truth, because there is no truth in him. When he speaketh a lie, he speaketh of his own: for he is a liar, and the father of it.

Holiness

*2 Corinthians 7:1 - Having therefore these promises, dearly beloved, let us cleanse ourselves from all filthiness of the flesh and spirit, perfecting holiness in the fear of God.

---

*1 Thessalonians 4:7 - For God hath not called us unto uncleanness, but unto holiness.

---

*Hebrews 12:14 - Follow peace with all [men], and holiness, without which no man shall see the Lord:

---

*Leviticus 19:2 - Speak unto all the congregation of the children of Israel, and say unto them, Ye shall be holy: for I the LORD your God [am] holy.

*Isaiah 35:8 - And an highway shall be there, and a way, and it shall be called The way of holiness; the unclean shall not pass over it; but it [shall be] for those: the wayfaring men, though fools, shall not err [therein].

---

*1 Thessalonians 5:23 - And the very God of peace sanctify you wholly; and [I pray God] your whole spirit and soul and body be preserved blameless unto the coming of our Lord Jesus Christ.

---

*James 1:21 - Wherefore lay apart all filthiness and superfluity of naughtiness, and receive with meekness the engrafted word, which is able to save your souls.

---

*1 John 3:3 - And every man that hath this hope in him purifieth himself, even as he is pure.

---

*Hebrews 12:10 - For they verily for a few days chastened [us] after their own pleasure; but he for [our] profit, that [we] might be partakers of his holiness.

---

*1 Corinthians 15:34 - Awake to righteousness, and sin not; for some have not the knowledge of God: I speak [this] to your shame.

---

*1 Corinthians 6:20 - For ye are bought with a price: therefore glorify God in your body, and in your spirit, which are God's.

---

*1 John 1:7 - But if we walk in the light, as he is in the light, we have fellowship one with another, and the blood of Jesus Christ his Son cleanseth us from all sin.

---

*1 Timothy 6:6 - But godliness with contentment is great gain.

---

*Matthew 5:8 - Blessed [are] the pure in heart: for they shall see God.

---

*Matthew 5:6 - Blessed [are] they which do hunger and thirst after righteousness: for they shall be filled.

ABOUT THE AUTHOR

Dr. Michael and Kathleen Yeager have served as pastors/apostles, missionaries, evangelist, broadcasters and authors for almost four decades. Up to this time they have authored ten books. Their three son, daughter and daughter in law work with them in the ministry. Michael and Kathleen have been married sense 1978. They have helped start over 27 churches. They flow in the gifts of the Holy Spirit, teaching the word of God, with wonderful signs following and confirming God's word. In 1983 they began Jesus is Lord Ministries international. The same year the Lord spoke to Dr. Yeager to go on TV. From then to now they have been actively involved in broadcast media for the propagation of the gospel.

Jesus is Lord Ministries International
3425 Chambersburg Rd.

Made in the USA
Middletown, DE
04 May 2015